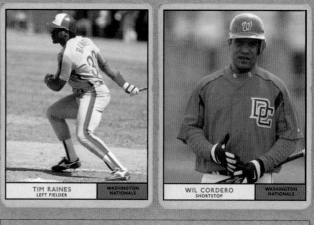

TIM RAINES
LEFT FIELDER

WASHINGTON
NATIONALS

WIL CORDERO
SHORTSTOP

WASHINGTON
NATIONALS

THE STORY OF THE WASHINGTON NATIONALS

Published by Creative Education
P.O. Box 227, Mankato, Minnesota 56002
Creative Education is an imprint of The Creative Company
www.thecreativecompany.us

Design and production by Blue Design
Art direction by Rita Marshall
Printed by Corporate Graphics in the United States of America

Photographs by Getty Images (Al Bello, Andrew D. Bernstein, Bernstein Associates, David Boily/MLB Photos, Ricky Carioti/The Washington Post, Kevin C. Cox, Jonathan Daniel, Jonathan Daniel/Allsport, Diamond Images, G Flume, FPG, Jose Jimenez/Primera Hora, Jonathan Kirn/Allsport, Mitchell Layton, Mitchell Layton/MLB Photos, John McDonnell/The Washington Post, National Baseball Hall of Fame Library/MLB Photos, Vito Palmisano, Rich Pilling/MLB Photos, Joe Robbins, Arnold Sachs, Ezra Shaw, Robert Skeoch/MLB Photos, Ron Vesely/MLB Photos)

Library of Congress Cataloging-in-Publication Data

Goodman, Michael E.
The story of the Washington Nationals / by Michael E. Goodman.
p. cm. — (Baseball: the great American game)
Includes index.
Summary: The history of the Washington Nationals professional baseball team from its inaugural 1969 season as the Montreal Expos to today, spotlighting the team's greatest players and most memorable moments.
ISBN 978-1-60818-060-8
1. Washington Nationals (Baseball team)—History—Juvenile literature. I. Title. II. Series.

GV875.W27G66 2011
796.357'6409753—dc22   2010025480

CPSIA: 110310 PO1381

First Edition
9 8 7 6 5 4 3 2 1

Page 3: Outfielder Jose Guillen
Page 4: Outfielder Willie Harris

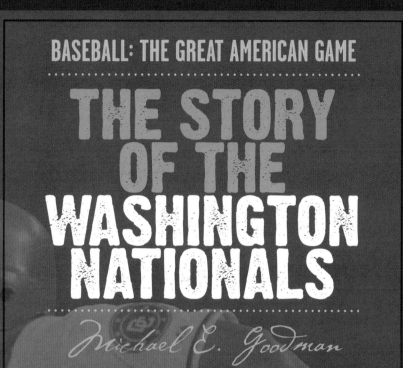

BASEBALL: THE GREAT AMERICAN GAME

THE STORY OF THE WASHINGTON NATIONALS

Michael E. Goodman

CREATIVE EDUCATION

CONTENTS

A CAPITAL IDEA

etween 1776 and 1790, the United States' capital circulated among the cities of Philadelphia, Baltimore, York, Princeton, Annapolis, Trenton, and New York. Finally, in 1790, the U.S. Congress decided the country needed a permanent capital that was not part of any one state. President George Washington, a surveyor by trade, carved out a diamond-shaped district that included parts of Maryland and Virginia. After 10 years of planning and building, the new capital was ready for occupancy in 1800. At the suggestion of then president John Adams, the city was named Washington in honor of the former president, who had died the year before.

As the U.S. government grew, so did Washington. By 1900, it was the country's 15th-largest city, with a population nearing 280,000. So it seemed logical that when professional baseball's American League (AL) was formed in 1901, a franchise would be established in Washington. Management debated whether to name the team the Senators or the Nationals before settling on Senators. That franchise

Washington, D.C., features numerous distinctive landmarks, including the Washington Monument (at left) and the Lincoln Memorial (below).

PITCHER · STEVE ROGERS

A crafty right-handed starter, Rogers is widely regarded as the best pitcher in Expos history. A late bloomer, he didn't even play baseball until his senior year in high school. Rogers spent his entire 13-year career with the Expos, winning 158 games. While he was never able to win 20 games in a single season, he did win 19 games in 1982 and posted winning records in 8 seasons. Rogers will forever be remembered as the man who gave up the series-winning homer to the Los Angeles Dodgers' Rick Monday in the 1981 NL Championship Series (NLCS), but his accomplishments as an Expos player spoke for themselves.

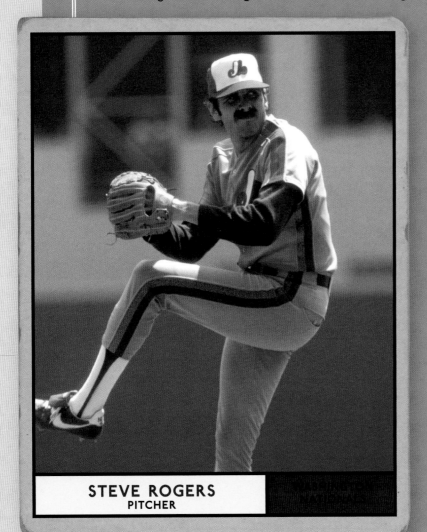

STEVE ROGERS
PITCHER

STATS

Expos seasons: 1973–85

Height: 6-foot-1

Weight: 182

- **129 complete games**
- **37 complete-game shutouts**
- **158–152 career record**
- **5-time All-Star**

eventually moved to Minnesota and was replaced by another Senators club that later relocated to Texas. Washington fans were without a home team from 1972 until 2004, when the owners of the Montreal Expos decided to relocate their team south of the Canadian border and rename it the Nationals.

By the time the Nationals took the field in Washington, the Expos had already built a 36-season history in Montreal. The club was established as part of Major League Baseball's expansion in 1969 and took its name from an impressive world's fair held two years earlier in Montreal—the Exposition, or "Expo" for short. The club became an immediate hit with Montreal fans, most of whom spoke French, who proudly called the Expos players "Nos Amours," which is French for "our beloveds."

The Expos built their first roster mostly with young unknowns and aging veterans, including starting pitchers Dan McGinn and Bill Stoneman, third baseman Jose "Coco" Laboy, and second baseman Gary Sutherland. Commanding this ragtag roster was veteran skipper Gene Mauch, known as the "Little General." Mauch was a disciplined man who worked his players hard during their first spring training. "At the end of each day, I felt like an old sock in a washing machine," grumbled one tired veteran.

The players might have been exhausted, but they looked fresh and colorful on the field. They wore bright red, white, and blue caps and uniforms with a fancy, multicolored "M" sewn on the front. Things became even more colorful in Montreal when team owners traded with the Houston Astros for right fielder Rusty Staub. The outfielder's fiery red hair quickly earned him the nickname "Le Grand Orange" from the French-speaking fans, and his outgoing nature made him an instant hero in Montreal.

Le Grand Orange and the Expos kicked off their first season with drama. Facing the Mets in New York on April 8, 1969, Laboy, McGinn, and Staub all belted home runs to highlight a wild 11–10 opening-day win. The club won its home opener in rickety Jarry Park a week later in a game almost postponed because of snow on the ground. Three nights later, Stoneman warmed up Montreal fans by tossing a no-hitter against the Philadelphia Phillies.

Rusty Staub spent 23 years in the majors. He made a respectable run at the hallowed mark of 3,000 career hits (finishing with 2,716), and he was just the second big-leaguer ever to hit a home run before turning 20 years old and after 40.

BASEBALL IN WASHINGTON

The Nationals were not the first big-league team based in Washington. From 1901 to 1961, a team alternately called the Senators and Nationals was part of the American League (AL). Because the club finished in last place four times in its first nine seasons, fans developed a saying connecting the city and its team: "Washington: First in war, first in peace, and last in the American League." The emergence of Hall of Fame pitcher Walter Johnson became the catalyst the team needed to escape from the cellar, and in both 1912 and 1913, the Senators finished in second place. In 1924, Johnson and 27-year-old second baseman/manager Bucky Harris propelled the club to a surprising world championship—the only one in franchise history. Over the next decade, the Senators won two more AL pennants, but from 1934 to 1960, they recorded only four winning seasons. The team's lack of success prompted ownership to relocate the franchise to Minneapolis in 1961, creating the Minnesota Twins, but an expansion franchise also known as the Senators was immediately awarded to Washington. For 10 years, the new Senators struggled to build a fan base, and after the 1971 season, they relocated to Dallas and became the Texas Rangers.

CATCHER · GARY CARTER

Nicknamed "The Kid" because of his youthful appearance and exuberance, Gary Carter burst onto the major-league scene in 1974 as an outfielder/catcher. A two-year captain of his high school football, basketball, and baseball teams, Carter was a born leader and was named *The Sporting News'* Rookie of the Year in 1975 after belting 17 home runs and driving in 68 runs. He became the Expos' full-time catcher in 1977 and quickly established himself as one of the game's best backstops—both offensively and defensively. "He had a rocket arm, and he was always hustle, hustle, hustle," said Mets first baseman Keith Hernandez.

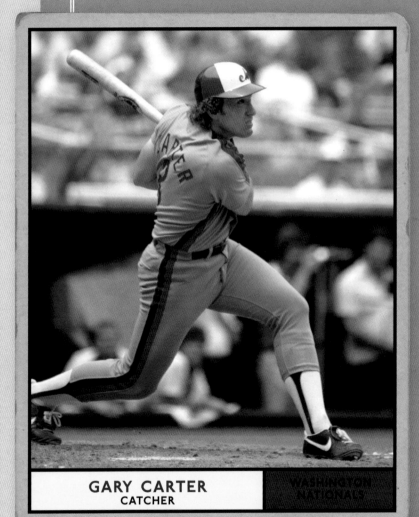

GARY CARTER
CATCHER

STATS

Expos seasons: 1974–84, 1992

Height: 6-foot-2

Weight: 215

- **324 career HR**

- **3-time Gold Glove winner**

- **11-time All-Star**

- **Baseball Hall of Fame inductee (2003)**

FIRST BASEMAN · ANDRES GALARRAGA

Andres Galarraga was a popular player throughout a career that took him to seven different major-league teams and saw him return to the game after a bout with cancer. Nicknamed "The Big Cat" for his extraordinary quickness despite his large frame, Galarraga was an incredible fielder and a solid hitter. While his best offensive seasons were with the Colorado Rockies, Galarraga never forgot the team that gave him his start in baseball. In 2002, he returned to the Expos as a part-time player, giving Montreal fans a second chance to see one of their all-time favorites in action.

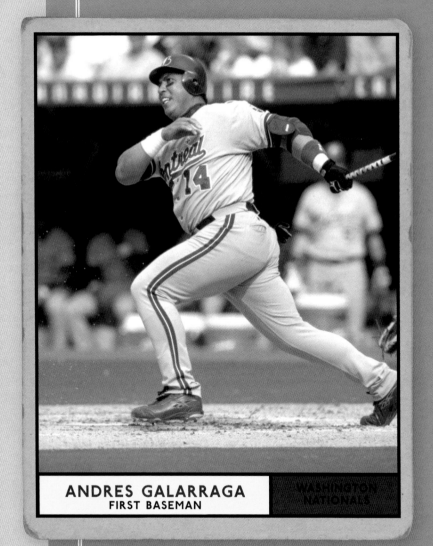

ANDRES GALARRAGA
FIRST BASEMAN

WASHINGTON NATIONALS

STATS

Expos seasons: 1985–91, 2002

Height: 6-foot-3

Weight: 235

- **1,425 career RBI**

- **399 career HR**

- **5-time All-Star**

- **2-time Gold Glove winner**

Still, like most expansion teams, the Expos struggled in their inaugural season, finishing with a 52–110 record. Mauch was not satisfied. Before the next season, he predicted that the Expos would "win 70 in '70." They did better than that. Thanks to Staub's timely hitting and 18 victories by rookie pitching sensation Carl Morton, the Expos finished with 73 wins.

The Expos made several key changes in the early 1970s, hoping to build a contender. First, Staub was traded to the Mets for three solid, everyday players—outfielder Ken Singleton, shortstop Tim Foli, and first baseman Mike Jorgensen. Then rookie pitcher Steve Rogers was brought up to the majors. In 1973, these new Expos helped Montreal challenge for the NL Eastern Division title until the last weekend of the season. "Wait until next year," promised Mauch. "These guys are just getting started."

NATIONALS

PUSHING FOR THE PLAYOFFS

 ver the next few seasons, the Expos reached into their minor-league system and promoted more talented young players to the major-league club. The first to make their way north in 1974 were third baseman Larry Parrish and outfielder/catcher Gary Carter. Parrish, a solid clutch hitter, had a way of turning opposing pitchers' mistakes into majestic home runs. Carter was nicknamed "The Kid" because of his youthful looks and enthusiasm, but he had grown-up talent. In 1975, he was named to the NL All-Star team as an outfielder. (Before his career was over, Carter would make 10 more All-Star Game appearances as a catcher.) Carter backed up his talent with a strong will to succeed. "If you put your mind to it, you can achieve what you want," he said. "Ambition has always been a great motivating force in my life."

Carter's career took a major turn in 1977 when new manager Dick Williams named him the Expos' full-time catcher. Carter developed into

Fourteen years after his major-league career came to a close, Andre Dawson entered the Hall of Fame as the sole inductee in the 2010 class.

ANDRE DAWSON

SECOND BASEMAN · DELINO DESHIELDS

After his senior year in high school, Delino Deshields had a big decision to make—to either play college basketball at Villanova University or major league baseball for Montreal. Luckily for the Expos, he chose baseball. A left-handed hitter and a right-handed fielder, he used his lively legs to quickly advance through the Expos' minor-league system, making his major-league debut in 1990. Deshields finished in the league's top 10 in stolen bases 10 times, stealing a career-high 56 bags in 1991. After the 1993 season, Deshields was dealt to the Dodgers for ace pitcher Pedro Martinez.

DELINO DESHIELDS
SECOND BASEMAN

WASHINGTON NATIONALS

STATS

Expos seasons: 1990–93

Height: 6-foot-1

Weight: 170

• 1997 NL leader in triples (14)

• .268 career BA

• 463 career stolen bases

• 872 career runs scored

a steady leader on the field and an outstanding hitter. Andre Dawson was promoted to take Carter's place in the outfield, and he finished his first season in Montreal with 19 homers, 21 stolen bases, and the NL Rookie of the Year award. Dawson also patrolled center field in Olympic Stadium (the Expos' new home) like a giant bird of prey, earning him the nickname "The Hawk."

With the Kid and the Hawk leading the way, the Expos climbed steadily up the NL East ladder, reaching second place in 1979. Montreal fans began chanting "Vive les Expos" ("Long live the Expos") as they prepared for the 1980 season and what they hoped would be a championship year at last.

Montreal got off to a fast start in 1980, with Carter and Dawson knocking in run after run and pitchers Steve Rogers and Scott Sanderson dominating opponents. The Expos went into the final weekend of the season tied with the Phillies for the division lead. The two teams faced off in Montreal in a three-game series, and Philadelphia won twice, silencing the crowd and Montreal's postseason ambitions.

The Expos gunned for the playoffs again in 1981. Rookie outfield sensation Tim "Rock" Raines joined the lineup and quickly established himself as an excellent leadoff hitter and base stealer. Because the 1981 season was shortened by a players' strike, it was divided into two halves. The Phillies won the first half of the season, while the Expos posted the NL East's best record in the second half. The Expos then defeated the Phillies in a special division playoff series, avenging the disappointing second-place finishes of the previous two years.

The Expos then faced off against the Los Angeles Dodgers in a hotly contested NLCS. After splitting the first four games, the teams were tied 1–1 in the bottom of the ninth inning of the deciding Game 5 when Williams summoned Rogers from the bullpen to shut down the Dodgers and give his team a chance to win the game in extra innings. Unfortunately, Dodgers outfielder Rick Monday hit a Rogers delivery out of the park to win the series. "It was a hanging slider," Rogers explained to reporters after the game. "I wanted it to break down and away, but it didn't." While the Dodgers went on to win the World Series, Expos fans were left to speak dejectedly of the day they would always remember as "Blue Monday."

HAIL TO THE CHIEF

On April 14, 1910, the Washington Senators opened their season with 12,000 fans in attendance. Among those fans was William Taft, the 27th president of the U.S. Prior to the game, umpire Billy Evans walked over to the president, handed him a ball, and instructed him to throw out the ceremonial first pitch from his seat. Taft threw the ball to starting pitcher Walter Johnson and stayed for the entire game, watching Johnson pitch a one-hit shutout. President Taft started a tradition of the nation's "chief" attending opening day in the capital city. Prior to the Senators' move to Texas in 1972, each president after Taft attended opening day at least once. Presidents Taft and Woodrow Wilson brought good luck to the Senators; the team went a combined 5–0 in games they attended. On the other hand, presidents Richard Nixon and Lyndon Johnson brought only bad luck, as the Senators went 0–5 with them in the stands. When the Nationals played their first home opener in Washington on April 14, 2005, president George W. Bush was on hand to throw out the first pitch at RFK Stadium, the old home of the Senators. The Nationals defeated the Arizona Diamondbacks that day, 5–3.

NATIONALS

OPTIMISM AND FRUSTRATION

s the 1982 season began, the city of Montreal was firmly behind its talented team. One optimistic hometown sportswriter confidently declared, "We're the team of the '80s. With Carter, Dawson, Raines, and Rogers, what can go wrong?" Unfortunately, over the next couple of seasons, the Expos would find that plenty could—and would—go wrong, as a series of injuries and bad trades kept the team from reaching its true potential.

Still, there were plenty of individual highlights in Montreal. In 1982, first baseman Al Oliver hit .331 and became the first Expos player to win the NL batting title. Two years later, first baseman Pete Rose joined the Expos and collected hit number 4,000 on his way to breaking the legendary Ty Cobb's longstanding record for career hits. Fireballing relief pitcher Jeff Reardon also began a string of impressive seasons as the team's closer in the early '80s and garnered two All-Star Game selections.

THIRD BASEMAN · RYAN ZIMMERMAN

With his sure hands in the field and strong hands at bat, Ryan Zimmerman quickly established himself as a star when he arrived in Washington near the end of the 2005 season, the club's first as the Nationals. He stroked a hit in his second major-league at bat and batted nearly .400 during his brief September debut. The next year, he took over the important third spot in the club's lineup for good and became the team's best run producer. In 2009, he won both a Gold Glove award for his fielding and a Silver Slugger award as the league's top-hitting third-sacker.

RYAN ZIMMERMAN
THIRD BASEMAN

WASHINGTON NATIONALS

STATS

Nationals seasons: 2005–present

Height: 6-foot-3

Weight: 230

- 116 career HR

- 449 career RBI

- 2009 All-Star

- 2009 Gold Glove winner

DENNIS MARTINEZ

EL PERFECTO

A perfect game is defined in major league baseball as a game in which a pitcher throws a complete-game victory that lasts a minimum of nine innings and in which no opposing player reaches first base. A perfect game is widely considered the pinnacle of pitching performance and is one of the most difficult feats to achieve in all of baseball—if not in any sport. Of course, a pitcher has to be at the top of his game, but he also has to rely on his defense not to make any errors and occasionally to make a great fielding play. On July 28, 1991, Dennis "El Presidente" Martinez of the Expos stepped on the mound to face the Los Angeles Dodgers in Dodger Stadium. From the start, Martinez had his best stuff. Inning after inning, he mowed the Dodgers down, one after another. By the seventh inning, Dodgers fans began to realize that they might be witnessing history, and the stands began to buzz as Martinez set about retiring the last nine batters. On his 95th pitch, he recorded the 27th and final out for a perfect game. Martinez became only the 13th pitcher in major-league history to be "perfect."

In 1985, Expos management decided to shake things up. Carter was traded to the Mets, and first baseman Andres "The Big Cat" Galarraga and veteran pitcher Dennis Martinez were brought in to fill the leadership void that Carter left behind. Despite their efforts, the team's record hovered near the .500 mark for the rest of the decade.

A major Montreal turnaround began in the early 1990s with the arrival of two natives of the Dominican Republic: veteran manager Felipe Alou, who arrived in 1992, and brash young pitcher Pedro Martinez, who came to town in 1994. Alou's patience and determination were just what the young, inexperienced Expos needed. The club recorded 87 wins in 1992 and 94 the next season. Although the Expos narrowly missed the playoffs both years, the team appeared ready to finally reach its first World Series.

As the 1994 season unfolded, Montreal, now featuring the overpowering fastball of Martinez, made clear that it was the team to beat in the NL. In late June, the red-hot Expos swept a series against the Atlanta Braves to take over first place in the NL East. They stayed on top for the remainder of the season, led by two talented outfielders: Moises Alou (Felipe's son) and Canadian-born Larry Walker. On the mound,

Martinez dominated the opposition, and closer John Wetteland was among the league's saves leaders.

The Expos were riding high atop the NL until August 12, when major-league players went on strike. After weeks of fruitless negotiations between players and owners, the season was canceled. With that, the Expos' fate was sealed: the 1994 team—the finest in franchise history—would never have the chance to prove itself in the postseason. "A lot of things about the strike hurt," said Walker. "But having that great season wasted is something I don't think I'll ever get over."

Over the next three seasons, Martinez continued to put up amazing numbers. He earned the NL Cy Young Award as the league's best pitcher in 1997 when he won 17 games, maintained an amazing 1.90 earned run average (ERA), and struck out 305 batters. Sadly, Martinez's career in Montreal would soon end, however, when economic pressures forced Montreal—one of baseball's smallest markets—to trade its star hurler to the Boston Red Sox after the season.

Luckily, 1998 brought a new fan favorite to Montreal—right fielder Vladimir Guerrero, a free-swinging slugger who wowed fans with

Vladimir Guerrero was one the rare big-league hitters to take his swings barehanded, without the use of batting gloves. His method clearly worked; as of 2010, he had posted 12 seasons with 25 or more home runs.

SHORTSTOP · WIL CORDERO

Cordero was scouted in Puerto Rico and signed by the Expos at the age of 16. Four years later, in 1992, he was called up to the big leagues after the midseason All-Star break. As a rookie, he overcame a variety of injuries to hit .302 in 45 games. In the strike-shortened 1994 season, the versatile shortstop had one of his best years as a major-leaguer, but he was then traded away after the 1995 season. When Cordero returned to play with the Expos and then the Nationals later in his career, he did so as a left fielder and a first baseman.

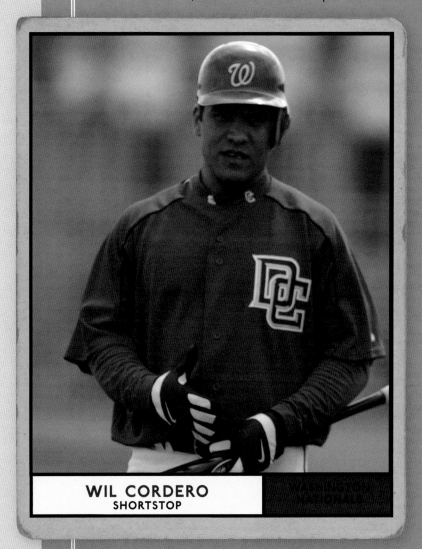

WIL CORDERO
SHORTSTOP

STATS

Expos/Nationals seasons: 1992–95, 2002–03, 2005

Height: 6-foot-2

Weight: 190

- **122 career HR**

- **566 career RBI**

- **.273 career BA**

- **1994 All-Star**

his explosive bat and rocket throwing arm. "He has all the tools to be outstanding, especially that arm," said Expos general manager Jim Beattie. "That's what people 'ooh' and 'ahh' about." But Guerrero was now the only real threat in the Expos' lineup, and the team plummeted toward the bottom of the NL East.

CROSSING THE BORDER

 s the new century began, the young Expos continued to stumble. Montreal fans cheered loudly for new stars such as slick-fielding shortstop Orlando Cabrera, hard-hitting second baseman Jose Vidro, and power pitcher Javier Vazquez. However, the team's youth and inconsistency led to an abundance of losses, costing Alou his job as manager. When Jeff Torborg took over as skipper, his mission was to return the Expos to respectability, but it would be a long, difficult road.

All of the losing had hurt the team's ability to draw fans, and the franchise was in serious financial trouble. After the 2001 season, rumors began to spread that Major League Baseball might contract—

LEFT FIELDER · TIM RAINES

Nicknamed "Rock" because of his chiseled physique, Tim Raines quickly established himself as one of the game's best leadoff hitters, causing Atlanta pitcher Rick Mahler to call him "the best offensive player in the league besides [Braves All-Star outfielder] Dale Murphy." In 1981, Raines was an integral part of the only Expos team ever to make it to the postseason.

In just 88 games that year, he stole an incredible 71 bases, and by 1984, he had become the first player ever to steal 70 bases in 4 consecutive seasons. A fan favorite, Raines was a fixture in the Expos' lineup for 13 years.

TIM RAINES
LEFT FIELDER

WASHINGTON NATIONALS

STATS

Expos seasons: 1979–90, 2001

Height: 5-foot-8

Weight: 178

- **1987 All-Star Game MVP**

- **808 career stolen bases**

- **1,571 career runs scored**

- **7-time All-Star**

OH, CANADA!

In an attempt to increase fan interest in the game, Major League Baseball decided to add interleague games to the regular season in 1997. This meant that teams from the NL would be pitted against teams from the AL. Previously, the only times a team from the NL could meet a team from the AL were in spring training exhibition games or in the World Series. When the schedule was announced, among the marquee matchups were the New York Mets against the New York Yankees, the Chicago Cubs against the Chicago White Sox, and the Montreal Expos against the Toronto Blue Jays. For the first time ever, two big-league teams from outside the U.S. would be playing the game known as "America's pastime." For this reason, "Oh, Canada!," not the U.S. national anthem, was sung before the game. When the Blue Jays hosted the Expos on June 30, 1997, fans flooded SkyDome in Toronto to see which Canadian team was better. The Expos won the first two games by an identical 2–1 score. The Blue Jays won the last game 7–6, but the Expos won the series, giving them bragging rights throughout Canada.

NATIONALS

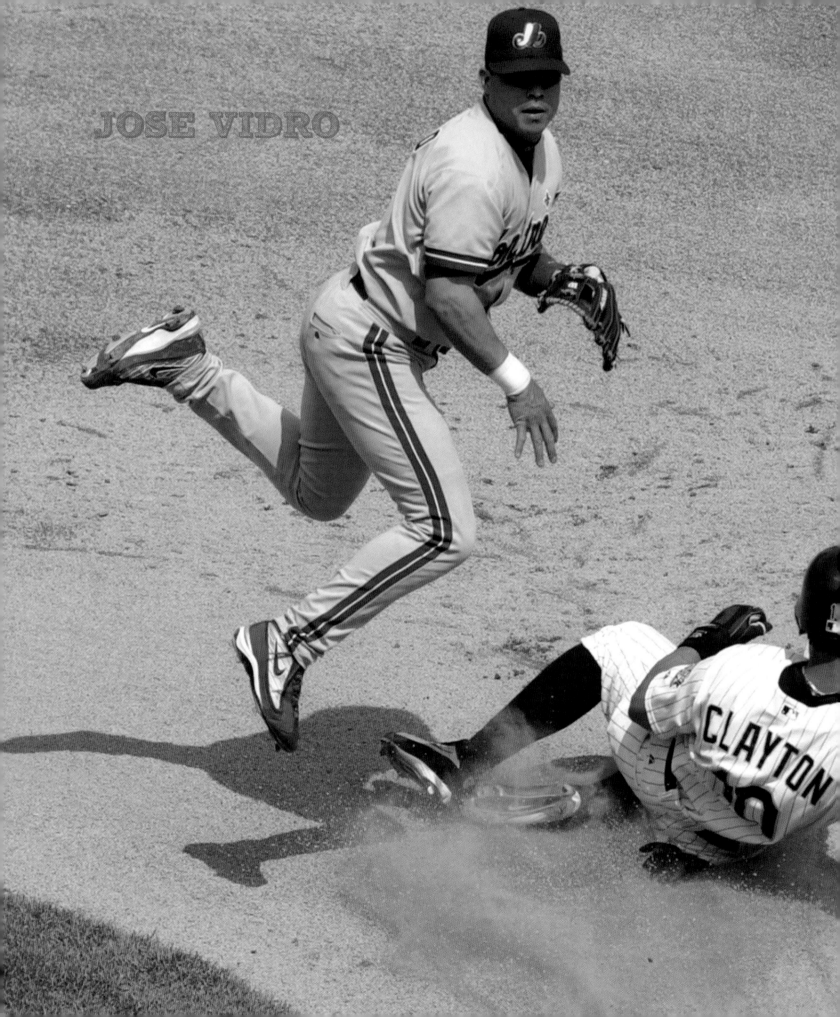
JOSE VIDRO

or eliminate—the Expos and the Minnesota Twins, two of the least profitable franchises. Even though the threats of contraction never materialized, the league did assume ownership of the Expos, bringing in Omar Minaya as baseball's first-ever Latino general manager and Frank Robinson as the club's manager. Although many people doubted the Expos would remain in Montreal, Minaya and Robinson never doubted that they could improve the team.

Guerrero and Vidro helped the Expos get off to a hot start in 2002. With a division title within reach, Minaya pulled off two key midseason trades for big pitcher Bartolo Colón and veteran outfielder Cliff Floyd. The recharged Expos battled the Atlanta Braves for the NL East title deep into the season before fading to an 83–79 finish—their first winning season in five years. They matched that record in 2003, too, but attendance continued to fall in Montreal, and baseball officials announced that the Expos would move south after the 2004 season. On October 3, 2004, Montreal lost to the Mets, 8–1, in what would be the team's last game as the Expos. By the time the 2005 season began, the team had been transformed into the Washington Nationals.

The return of baseball to the U.S. capital was a resounding success. It had been 34 years since the Senators left Washington for Texas, and the city's baseball-starved citizens were ready to embrace a new team. Still, not much was expected of Robinson's squad, especially after the Nationals lost the season opener 8–4 to the Phillies. "There was no pageantry today for the D.C. Nationals," said reliever Joey Eischen. "We came here to kick some butt—and we didn't. But we'll be out there again on Wednesday, and we're going to bring it."

After losing that first game, the team "brought it" to the rest of the NL, soon sprinting to first place in the NL East. The off-season acquisition of right fielder Jose Guillen, who finished the year with 24 home runs, provided a valuable middle-of-the-lineup threat to opposing pitchers. While promising rookie outfielder Ryan Church helped carry the offensive load, workhorse hurler Livan Hernandez won 15 games and led the major leagues in innings pitched. Perhaps the biggest surprise, though, was Chad Cordero, a second-year closer who blazed his way to a league-leading 47 saves.

As the 2005 season progressed, the Nationals remained in the playoff hunt. Robinson established high expectations

CENTER FIELDER · ANDRE DAWSON

Andre Dawson was one of the best all-around players ever to wear a Montreal uniform. In the early 1980s, the Expos enjoyed some of their most successful seasons when "The Hawk" patrolled center field with his fast legs and sure glove. At the plate, Dawson was a free and dangerous swinger. "When he's hot, there's no stopping him," said Hall of Fame hurler Nolan Ryan. "He'll even hit a ball over his head to beat you." Dawson combined power and speed and is the only Expos player to have hit more than 200 home runs and stolen more than 200 bases.

STATS

Expos seasons: 1976–86

Height: 6-foot-3

Weight: 195

- **1987 NL MVP**

- **438 career HR**

- **8-time All-Star**

- **Baseball Hall of Fame inductee (2010)**

ANDRE DAWSON
CENTER FIELDER

WASHINGTON
NATIONALS

for his players and stressed the importance of good fundamental play. The Nationals frequently struggled to score runs, but a mixture of good defense, pitching, and timely hitting enabled them to win many close games. With only two weeks left, Washington remained within striking distance of the NL Wild Card playoff berth. Although the Houston Astros ended up running away with the Wild Card, the 81–81 Nationals were one of the game's best success stories of 2005. "I think we did what we had to do to capture the imagination of the D.C. fans," said Robinson.

"THE PLAN" FOR THE FUTURE

 nfortunately, the Nationals could not maintain that impressive pace. One of the few players to capture the imagination of Washington fans over the next several years was dynamic third baseman Ryan Zimmerman. Zimmerman had provided an immediate sign of his talent and self-confidence in his second game in a Nationals uniform near

RYAN ZIMMERMAN

the end of the 2005 season, smacking a double in his second at bat. "They say your first hit is the hardest to get," the 20-year-old told reporters after the game. "I'm glad I didn't have to wait too long for mine." Zimmerman continued to pound the ball in 2006—his first full major-league season—when he batted .287, clubbed 20 homers, drove in 110 RBI, and placed a close second in the voting for NL Rookie of the Year.

Before the 2007 season, a new ownership group took over the Nationals and began shaking things up. Stan Kasten was brought in as general manager, and Manny Acta was hired as manager. Kasten was

SAN JUAN EXPOS

In 2001, the small-market Expos found themselves unable to compete financially with teams in bigger metropolitan areas such as New York, Chicago, and Los Angeles. As a result, Montreal fans found it difficult to support their losing team. In 2001, the Expos routinely drew fewer than 10,000 fans per game, averaging a woeful 7,935 fans for home games. Whispers that two teams would be contracted swirled throughout the majors. The Expos and the Minnesota Twins (another small-market team) appeared to be the leading candidates for elimination. On February 14, 2002, the league agreed not to contract any teams. Still, Major League Baseball looked into alternative ways to improve the Expos' attendance and revenue. In 2003, the team announced it would play 22 of its "home games" at Hiram Bithorn Stadium in San Juan, Puerto Rico. Fans in Puerto Rico flocked to the small stadium, largely to see the team's Latino stars such as Vladimir Guerrero and Jose Vidro. The games played in San Juan regularly outdrew the games played in Montreal. Thanks in large part to the Puerto Rico contests, the Expos were able to draw more than a million fans at "home" for the first time since 1998.

RIGHT FIELDER · VLADIMIR GUERRERO

When Vladimir Guerrero made his major-league debut in 1996, his raw skills included a superb throwing arm, speed, and pure slugging power. Still, many doubted that he would become a star because of his free-swinging approach at the plate. But Guerrero proved to his doubters that he could get hold of almost any pitch thrown to him. By 1998, he had established himself as one of the game's rising stars, and from then through 2003, he led the Expos in most offensive categories. After an injury-shortened 2003 season, Guerrero signed a free-agent contract with the Los Angeles Angels of Anaheim.

VLADIMIR GUERRERO
RIGHT FIELDER

WASHINGTON NATIONALS

STATS

Expos seasons: 1996–2003

Height: 6-foot-2

Weight: 218

- 436 career HR

- .320 career BA

- 2004 AL MVP

- 9-time All-Star

MANAGER · FELIPE ALOU

The Alou family was a baseball family, in both the Dominican Republic and the U.S. Felipe, along with younger brothers Jesús and Matty, began his major-league career with the San Francisco Giants, where the Alous made up the first all-brother outfield in 1963. After his playing days ended, Alou worked his way up the coaching ranks until 1992, when he was hired as the Expos' manager. Under Alou's guidance, the Expos emerged as World Series contenders during the early '90s, and Alou became the winningest manager in club history. After leaving Montreal in 2001, he went on to manage the Giants.

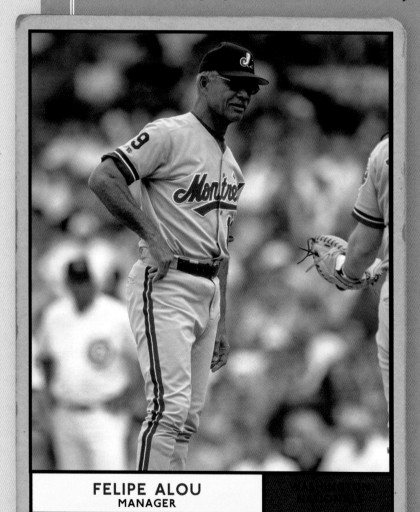

FELIPE ALOU
MANAGER

STATS

Expos seasons as manager: 1992–2001

Managerial record: 1,033–1,021

1994 NL Manager of the Year

well-respected for having built the Braves into an NL powerhouse in the 1990s and early 2000s. Now, he proposed what he called "The Plan" for rebuilding and restructuring every aspect of the Nationals franchise.

Before "The Plan" could be put in motion, however, the club suffered through a dismal 2007 season. Things started off badly in Washington that year and then got worse. On opening day, speedy shortstop Cristian Guzman pulled his hamstring and was lost for several weeks. Injuries also hit the team's pitching corps hard, and the club's record stood at 9–25 by mid-May. "Almost everything that could sink a team's attitude has befallen the Nationals," wrote one local reporter. Yet just as some writers were predicting that the Nationals might break the all-time record for losses in a season (120, set by the 1962 Mets), they began a winning streak. Behind the timely hitting of Zimmerman, Church, and second baseman Ronnie Belliard, Washington finished the year 73–89, two victories better than in 2006.

Washington started 2008 on a high note. On opening day, a standing-room-only crowd packed the brand-new Nationals Park, overlooking the U.S. Capitol, to watch the home team take on the Braves. President George

W. Bush threw out the ceremonial first pitch at the beginning of the game, and Zimmerman hit a walk-off homer to cap a thrilling 3–2 Washington victory. Unfortunately, that game proved to be a rare highlight, as the team would win only 58 more contests all year while losing 102.

The 2009 season saw more shakeups and changes in D.C. On the field, the big news was that Acta was fired and replaced by veteran skipper Jim Riggleman, who had grown up in the Washington suburbs and was a fan of the old Senators. Meanwhile, off the field, a milestone event in "The Plan" was reached when Kasten chose college pitching sensation Stephen Strasburg as the top overall pick in baseball's amateur draft and then signed him to a $15.9-million contract—a major-league record for draftees. The young standout's fastball regularly topped 100 miles per hour in college, and he could make a baseball dance. "Whenever you see a fastball at 100 miles per hour, it's always straight, no movement," noted one scout. "But his fastball cuts."

Even though the Nationals remained at the bottom of the NL East in both 2009 and 2010, their prospects began looking up. First, the club obtained Bryce Harper, a 17-year-old catcher/outfielder with phenomenal slugging

TEDDY'S WINLESS STREAK

In 2006, the Nationals began scheduling a promotional "Race of the Presidents" at every home game. In the middle of the fourth inning, runners dressed up in costumes representing presidents George Washington, Thomas Jefferson, Abraham Lincoln, and Teddy Roosevelt—the four leaders carved on Mount Rushmore—put on a spirited race to a finish line near the Nationals' dugout, while fans cheered them on. Jefferson won the most races in 2006, Washington in 2007, and Lincoln in both 2008 and 2009. In all four of those years, Teddy Roosevelt did not win a single race. Sometimes, Teddy would seem to win but would be disqualified for some infraction, such as riding a golf cart or rickshaw, descending a zip line to make a quick finish, or cutting corners on the course. Even when he took the lead, Teddy often caused his own undoing by stopping to "high-five" fans while the other runners passed him by. Soon many fans began wearing T-shirts or carrying signs that read "Let Teddy Win!" A rumor spread that Teddy would finally win on opening day in 2008 when the team moved into the new Nationals Park, but he faded in the stretch once again.

Stephen Strasburg showed electrifying stuff on the mound in 2010; in his major-league debut, he struck out a franchise-record 14 batters.

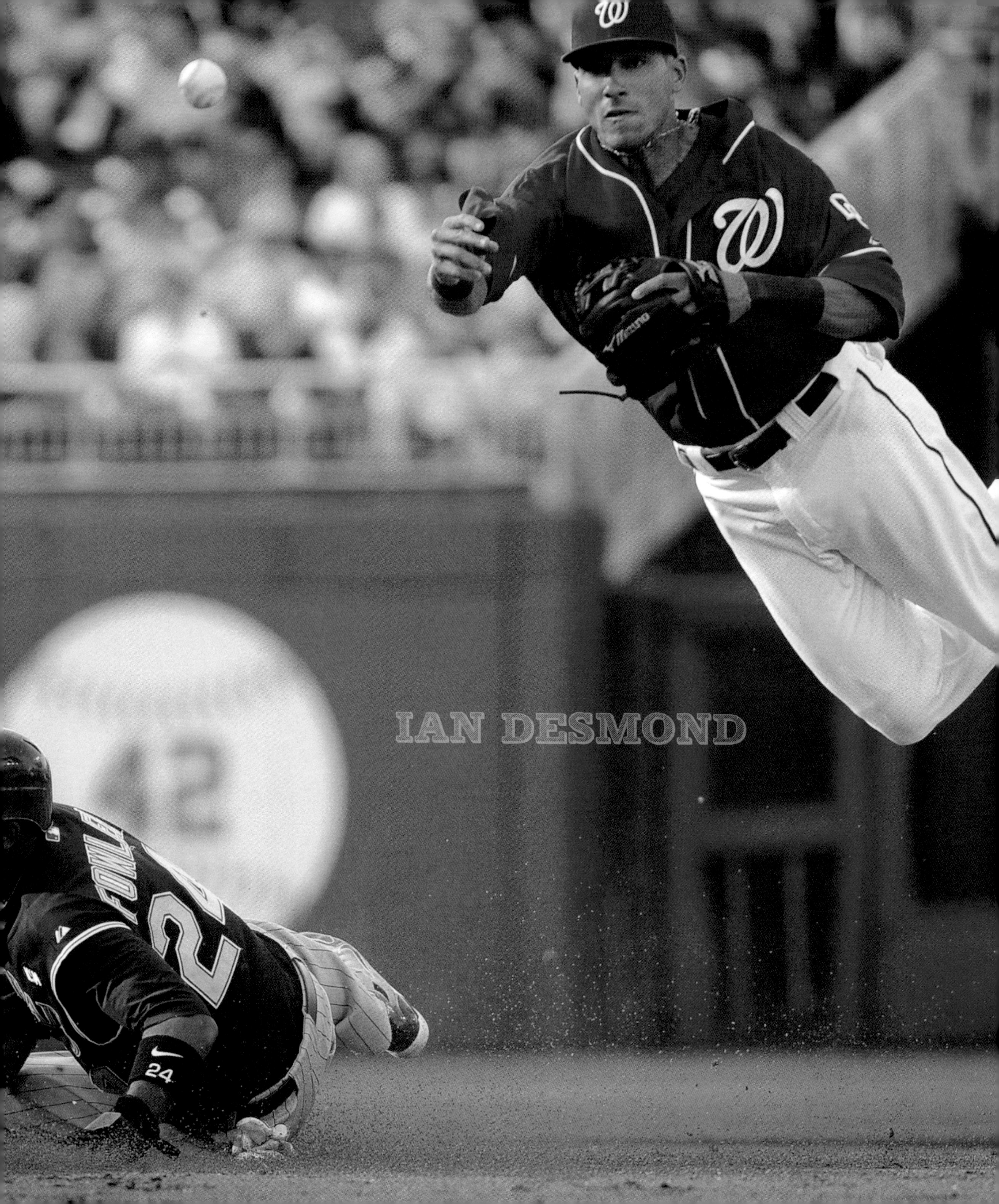

IAN DESMOND

Despite the efforts of quick shortstop Ian Desmond (opposite) and slugging first baseman Adam Dunn (below, right), the 2010 Nationals went just 69–93.

power, with the first overall pick in baseball's 2010 draft. Then, Strasburg became an instant star, blowing batters away before suffering an elbow injury that required surgery.

After spending 36 years north of the border, the Montreal Expos have found a new life in Washington, D.C. Today's Washington Nationals are out to make their own history in a city that is known for both making and preserving U.S. history. As they play amid such treasured landmarks as the Washington Monument and the Lincoln Memorial, Washington players are hoping to soon add some more impressive keepsakes to D.C.—an NL pennant and World Series trophy.

INDEX